FAVORITE
BASEBALL
★ TEAMS ★

BOSTON
RED SOX

BY K.C. KELLEY

The Child's World

Published by The Child's World®
1980 Lookout Drive • Mankato, MN 56003-1705
800-599-READ • www.childsworld.com

ACKNOWLEDGMENTS
The Child's World®: Mary Berendes,
    Publishing Director
The Design Lab: Kathleen Petelinsek, Design
Shoreline Publishing Group, LLC: James
    Buckley Jr., Production Director

PHOTOS
Cover: Focus on Baseball
Interior: All photos by Focus on Baseball except:
AP/Wide World: 5, 10, 17, 18, 22 (inset)
Baseball Hall of Fame: 22 main
Getty Images: 9

LIBRARY OF CONGRESS
CATALOGING-IN-PUBLICATION DATA
Kelley, K. C.
  Boston Red Sox / by K.C. Kelley.
    p. cm. — (Favorite baseball teams)
  Includes index.
  ISBN 978-1-60253-376-9 (library bound : alk. paper)
  1. Boston Red Sox (Baseball team)—History—
Juvenile literature. I. Title. II. Series.
  GV875.B62.K45 2010
  796.357'640974461—dc22   2009039445

Printed in the United States of America
Mankato, Minnesota
November 2009
F11460

On the cover: Dustin Pedroia,
Second Base

CONTENTS

Go, Red Sox!

The Boston Red Sox are one of baseball's most famous teams. For nearly one-hundred years they were famous for not winning the **World Series**. Their fans stayed **loyal**, though. In recent years, the Red Sox have been one of baseball's best teams. Let's meet the Red Sox!

"We did it!" Jonathan Papelbon and Jason Varitek celebrate winning ▶ the 2007 World Series.

Who Are the Red Sox?

The Boston Red Sox are a team in baseball's American League (A.L.). The A.L. joins with the National League to form Major League Baseball. The Red Sox play in the East Division of the A.L. The division winners get to play in the league playoffs. The playoff winners from the two leagues face off in the World Series. The Red Sox have won five World Series championships.

◀ Dustin Pedroia and Kevin Youkilis are top Red Sox hitters.

Where They Came From

The Boston Red Sox haven't always been the Red Sox. The team started in 1901. They were called the Americans until 1908. They have always played in Boston, however. From 1918 through 2003, they didn't win any World Series. In 2004, they finally won one!

Boston's Fred Lynn was safe in this play! Even so, the team lost to the ▶
Cincinnati Reds in this 1975 World Series.

Who They Play

The Boston Red Sox play 162 games each season. That includes about 14 games against the other teams in their division, the A.L. East. The Red Sox have won six A.L. East championships. The other East teams are the Baltimore Orioles, the New York Yankees, the Tampa Bay Rays, and the Toronto Blue Jays. The Red Sox and the Yankees are baseball's biggest **rivals**. Their games always get the fans charged up! These two teams have even battled in the playoffs. The Red Sox also play some teams from the National League. Their N.L. **opponents** change every year.

◀ J.D. Drew slides in safely, scoring another run for Boston against their main rival, the Yankees.

Where They Play

Fenway Park is baseball's oldest ballpark. It opened in 1912. Fans everywhere love Fenway for its old-time style. The outside is made of bricks. The left-field wall is 37 feet (11 m) tall, the biggest in baseball. The wall is called The Green Monster! Since 2006, fans have been able to sit above the Monster. Before every game, the streets around Fenway Park fill with fans. They eat hot dogs, buy **souvenirs**, and share their love of the Sox!

Those high-up fans in Fenway Park have a "Monster's-eye" view of the action! ▶

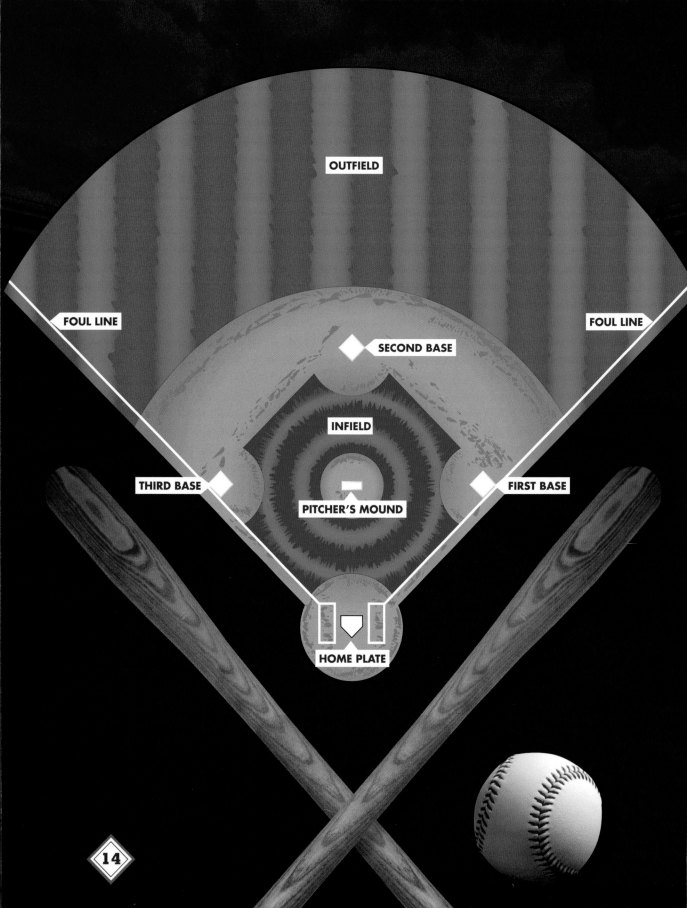

OUTFIELD

FOUL LINE

FOUL LINE

SECOND BASE

INFIELD

THIRD BASE

FIRST BASE

PITCHER'S MOUND

HOME PLATE

The Baseball Diamond

Baseball games are played on a diamond. Four bases form this diamond shape. The bases are 90 feet (27 m) apart. The area around the bases is called the **infield**. At the center of the infield is the pitcher's mound. The grass area beyond the bases is called the **outfield**. White lines start at **home plate** and go toward the outfield. These are the foul lines. Baseballs hit outside these lines are out of play. The outfield walls are about 300–450 feet (91–137 m) from home plate.

Big Days!

The Red Sox have had some great seasons in their history. Here are three of them:

1918: The Red Sox won their third World Series in five years. They were led by Babe Ruth. The future home-run star was a great pitcher for Boston.

2004: After 86 years, the Red Sox finally won a World Series title. To reach the Series, they beat the rival Yankees in four straight games. Then they beat the St. Louis Cardinals to win the Series.

2007: They did it again! With top pitchers and great hitting, the Red Sox won another World Series. This time, they beat the Colorado Rockies.

After 86 years, the Red Sox finally danced on the field after the ▶ 2004 World Series.

Tough Days!

The Red Sox have had a lot of tough seasons. Here are three of the worst:

1946: The St. Louis Cardinals beat the Red Sox in Game 7 of the World Series. It was Boston's only chance in the World Series from 1918 until 1967.

1986: The Red Sox were one out away from winning the World Series. Then the New York Mets came from behind to win Games 6 and 7.

2003: The final game of the playoffs was a real battle. In the 12th inning, Aaron Boone hit a homer that won the game for the Yankees. The Yankees went to the World Series—and the Red Sox went home!

◀ A Yankee in a Red Sox book? That's the Yankees' Aaron Boone celebrating after knocking the Red Sox out of the 2003 playoffs.

Meet the Fans

The Red Sox play in Boston, but their fans live everywhere. So many people love the team that they are called the "Red Sox Nation." The six states in New England are packed with Sox fans. People who moved away from the area still follow the team, too. The Red Sox have sold out every game at Fenway Park for more than four years!

Fans fill Yawkey Way outside Fenway Park. The street was named ▶ for a former Red Sox owner.

Carl Yastrzemski, Outfield

Heroes Then . . .

Cy Young won 511 games, more than any other pitcher. He threw the first **perfect game** of the twentieth century. Tris Speaker was one of the best **defensive** outfielders ever. Babe Ruth was a famous slugger with the Yankees, but he began as a star pitcher for Boston. Ted Williams is called "the best hitter who ever lived." He hit .406 in 1941. No player has ever topped him. Carl "Yaz" Yastrzemski took over for Williams in left field. He was the first A.L. player with 3,000 hits and 400 homers. Jim Rice stepped in for Yaz and also had a **Hall of Fame** career. Pitcher Roger Clemens won three **Cy Young Awards** with the Sox.

◀ The great Ted Williams was one of the best hitters of all time. Inset: "Yaz" was a great hitter and a super fielder.

Heroes
Now . . .

Josh Beckett is one of baseball's best pitchers. He joined Boston in 2006 and helped them win the 2007 World Series. Second baseman Dustin Pedroia was the 2008 **Most Valuable Player (MVP)**. First baseman Kevin Youkilis won the **Hank Aaron Award** that year for top hitter. Outfielder Jacoby Ellsbury is a top base stealer. Slugger Jason Bay joined the team in 2009 and drove in more than 100 runs. David "Big Papi" Ortiz is a powerful hitter. The **closer** is Jonathon Papelbon. When he comes in, it's usually "game over" for the opponent!

Kevin Youkilis, First Base

Josh Beckett, Pitcher

Dustin Pedroia, Second Base

CATCHER'S CHEST PROTECTOR

TEAM JERSEY

"C" FOR TEAM CAPTAIN

UNDERSHIRT

CATCHER'S MITT

TEAM PANTS

CATCHER'S SHIN GUARDS

BASEBALL CLEATS

BAT

BATTING HELMET

BATTING GLOVES

Jason Bay, Outfield

Gearing Up

Baseball players all wear a team jersey and pants. They have to wear a team hat in the field and a helmet when batting. Take a look at Jason Varitek and Jason Bay to see some other parts of a baseball player's uniform.

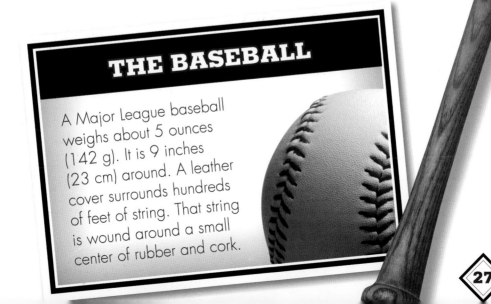

THE BASEBALL

A Major League baseball weighs about 5 ounces (142 g). It is 9 inches (23 cm) around. A leather cover surrounds hundreds of feet of string. That string is wound around a small center of rubber and cork.

27

SPORTS STATS

Here are some all-time career records for the Boston Red Sox. All the stats are through the 2009 season.

HOME RUNS

Ted Williams, 521
Carl Yastrzemski, 452

RUNS BATTED IN

Carl Yastrzemski, 1,844
Ted Williams, 1,839

BATTING AVERAGE

Ted Williams, .344
Wade Boggs, .338

WINS BY A PITCHER

Cy Young, 192

Roger Clemens, 192

STOLEN BASES

Harry Hooper, 300

Tris Speaker, 267

WINS BY A MANAGER

Joe Cronin, 1,071

EARNED RUN AVERAGE

Smokey Joe Wood, 1.97

Cy Young, 1.99

Glossary

closer a relief pitcher who comes in at the end of a game to "close out" a win for the team

Cy Young Award an award given to the top pitcher in each league

defensive trying to stop the other team from scoring

Hall of Fame a building in Cooperstown, New York, where baseball's greatest players are honored

Hank Aaron Award an award given to the top overall hitter in each league

home plate a five-sided rubber pad where batters stand to swing, and where runners touch base to score runs

infield the area around and between the four bases of a baseball diamond

loyal supporting something no matter what

manager the person who is in charge of the team and chooses who will bat and pitch

Most Valuable Player (MVP) a yearly award given to the top player in each league

opponents teams or players that play against each other

outfield the large, grass area beyond the infield of a baseball diamond

perfect game a game in which the winning pitcher doesn't allow any hitters to get on base

rivals teams that play each other often and have an ongoing competition

souvenirs something you keep to remind you of a place or an event (such as a baseball game)

World Series the Major League Baseball championship, played each year between the winners of the American and National Leagues

Find Out More

BOOKS

Buckley, James Jr. *Eyewitness Baseball*. New York: DK Publishing, 2010.

Stewart, Mark. *Boston Red Sox*. Chicago: Norwood House Press, 2008.

Teitelbaum, Michael. *Baseball*. Ann Arbor, MI: Cherry Lake Publishing, 2009.

WEB SITES

Visit our Web page for links about the Boston Red Sox and other pro baseball teams.

childsworld.com/links

Note to Parents, Teachers, and Librarians: We routinely verify our Web links to make sure they are safe, active sites—so encourage your readers to check them out!

Index

ABOUT THE AUTHOR

K.C. Kelley has written dozens of books on baseball and other sports for young readers. He has also been a youth baseball coach and called baseball games on the radio. His favorite team? The Boston Red Sox.